FRESHWATER AQUARIUM LOG BOOK

Name:

Phone:

E-Mail:

Address:

Date: 18/3/2022

☐ Mon ☐ Tue ☐ Wed ☐ Thu ☑ Fri ☐ Sat ☐ Sun

Time: 3pm

Freshwater Aquarium Log Book

Fish Info.

Fish Count: 6

Added Fish: —

Lost Fish: 0

Water Quality

Tank:

Water Type: Coldwater

Temp: 15 %

Change: ½ water level

PH Level

Ammonia:

Nitrite

Nitrite

Feeding & Light

Feeding Time		Light Time	
9	AM/~~PM~~	ON	AM/PM
9	~~AM~~/PM	OFF	AM/PM

Dosing

Supplements	Quantity
AQUA Safe	5ml

Other Tests

Notes

Tap water should be left at Room Temp.

2-3hrs before tank change

Sponge filter wash in water from tank change

Water change once a month.

Gravel hoover high traffic area

Ph test evening after water change

Freeze dried Daphnia flakes + 3 times week

Goldfish food flake once 2 a day.

Freeze dried Bloodworm flakes + 2 times week

Tetra Mini Granules once a day

Date: / /

☐ Mon ☐ Tue ☐ Wed ☐ Thu ☐ Fri ☐ Sat ☐ Sun

Time:

Water Quality

Tank :

Water Type :

Temp: %

Change:

PH Level

Ammonia:

Nitrite

Nitrite

Dosing

Supplements	Quantity

Freshwater Aquarium Log Book

Fish Info.

Fish Count :

Added Fish :

Lost Fish :

Feeding & Light

Feeding Time	Light Time
☐ AM/PM	ON AM/PM
☐ AM/PM	OFF AM/PM

Other Tests

Notes

Freshwater Aquarium Log Book

Date: / /

☐ Mon ☐ Tue ☐ Wed ☐ Thu ☐ Fri ☐ Sat ☐ Sun

Time:

Water Quality

Tank :
Water Type :
Temp: %
Change:
PH Level
Ammonia:
Nitrite
Nitrite

Dosing

Supplements	Quantity

Fish Info.

Fish Count :
Added Fish :
Lost Fish :

Feeding & Light

Feeding Time	Light Time
☐ AM/PM	ON AM/PM
☐ AM/PM	OFF AM/PM

Other Tests

Notes

Date: / /

☐ Mon ☐ Tue ☐ Wed ☐ Thu ☐ Fri ☐ Sat ☐ Sun

Time:

Water Quality

Tank :

Water Type :

Temp: %

Change:

PH Level

Ammonia:

Nitrite

Nitrite

Dosing

Supplements	Quantity

Freshwater Aquarium Log Book

Fish Info.

Fish Count :

Added Fish :

Lost Fish :

Feeding & Light

Feeding Time	Light Time
☐ AM/PM	ON AM/PM
☐ AM/PM	OFF AM/PM

Other Tests

Notes

Freshwater Aquarium Log Book

Date: / /

☐ Mon ☐ Tue ☐ Wed ☐ Thu ☐ Fri ☐ Sat ☐ Sun

Time:

Water Quality

Tank :

Water Type :

Temp: %

Change:

PH Level

Ammonia:

Nitrite

Nitrite

Dosing

Supplements	Quantity

Fish Info.

Fish Count :

Added Fish :

Lost Fish :

Feeding & Light

Feeding Time	Light Time
☐ AM/PM	ON AM/PM
☐ AM/PM	OFF AM/PM

Other Tests

Notes

Freshwater Aquarium Log Book

Date: / /

☐ Mon ☐ Tue ☐ Wed ☐ Thu ☐ Fri ☐ Sat ☐ Sun

Time:

Water Quality

Tank :

Water Type :

Temp: %

Change:

PH Level

Ammonia:

Nitrite

Nitrite

Dosing

Supplements	Quantity

Fish Info.

Fish Count :

Added Fish :

Lost Fish :

Feeding & Light

Feeding Time	Light Time
☐ AM/PM	ON AM/PM
☐ AM/PM	OFF AM/PM

Other Tests

Notes

Freshwater Aquarium Log Book

Date: / /

☐ Mon ☐ Tue ☐ Wed ☐ Thu ☐ Fri ☐ Sat ☐ Sun

Time:

Water Quality

Tank :

Water Type :

Temp: %

Change:

PH Level

Ammonia:

Nitrite

Nitrite

Dosing

Supplements	Quantity

Fish Info.

Fish Count :

Added Fish :

Lost Fish :

Feeding & Light

Feeding Time	Light Time
☐ AM/PM	ON AM/PM
☐ AM/PM	OFF AM/PM

Other Tests

Notes

Date: / /

☐ Mon ☐ Tue ☐ Wed ☐ Thu ☐ Fri ☐ Sat ☐ Sun

Time:

Water Quality

Tank :

Water Type :

Temp: %

Change:

PH Level

Ammonia:

Nitrite

Nitrite

Dosing

Supplements	Quantity

Freshwater Aquarium Log Book

Fish Info.

Fish Count :

Added Fish :

Lost Fish :

Feeding & Light

Feeding Time	Light Time
☐ AM/PM	ON AM/PM
☐ AM/PM	OFF AM/PM

Other Tests

Notes

Date: / /

☐ Mon ☐ Tue ☐ Wed ☐ Thu ☐ Fri ☐ Sat ☐ Sun

Time:

Water Quality

Tank :

Water Type :

Temp: %

Change:

PH Level

Ammonia:

Nitrite

Nitrite

Dosing

Supplements	Quantity

Freshwater Aquarium Log Book

Fish Info.

Fish Count :

Added Fish :

Lost Fish :

Feeding & Light

Feeding Time	Light Time
☐ AM/PM	ON AM/PM
☐ AM/PM	OFF AM/PM

Other Tests

Notes

Freshwater Aquarium Log Book

Date: / /

☐ Mon ☐ Tue ☐ Wed ☐ Thu ☐ Fri ☐ Sat ☐ Sun

Time:

Water Quality

Tank :
Water Type :
Temp: %
Change:
PH Level
Ammonia:
Nitrite
Nitrite

Dosing

Supplements	Quantity

Fish Info.

Fish Count :
Added Fish :
Lost Fish :

Feeding & Light

Feeding Time	Light Time
☐ AM/PM	ON AM/PM
☐ AM/PM	OFF AM/PM

Other Tests

Notes

Date: / /

☐ Mon ☐ Tue ☐ Wed ☐ Thu ☐ Fri ☐ Sat ☐ Sun

Time:

Water Quality

Tank :
Water Type :
Temp: %
Change:
PH Level
Ammonia:
Nitrite
Nitrite

Dosing

Supplements	Quantity

Freshwater Aquarium Log Book

Fish Info.

Fish Count :
Added Fish :
Lost Fish :

Feeding & Light

Feeding Time	Light Time
☐ AM/PM	ON AM/PM
☐ AM/PM	OFF AM/PM

Other Tests

Notes

Freshwater Aquarium Log Book

Date: / /

☐ Mon ☐ Tue ☐ Wed ☐ Thu ☐ Fri ☐ Sat ☐ Sun

Time:

Water Quality

Tank :

Water Type :

Temp: %

Change:

PH Level

Ammonia:

Nitrite

Nitrite

Dosing

Supplements	Quantity

Fish Info.

Fish Count :

Added Fish :

Lost Fish :

Feeding & Light

Feeding Time	Light Time
☐ AM/PM	ON AM/PM
☐ AM/PM	OFF AM/PM

Other Tests

Notes

Date: / /

☐ Mon ☐ Tue ☐ Wed ☐ Thu ☐ Fri ☐ Sat ☐ Sun

Time:

Water Quality

Tank :
Water Type :
Temp: %
Change:
PH Level
Ammonia:
Nitrite
Nitrite

Fish Info.

Fish Count :
Added Fish :
Lost Fish :

Feeding & Light

Feeding Time	Light Time
☐ AM/PM	ON AM/PM
☐ AM/PM	OFF AM/PM

Freshwater Aquarium Log Book

Dosing

Supplements	Quantity

Other Tests

Notes

Freshwater Aquarium Log Book

Date: / /

☐ Mon ☐ Tue ☐ Wed ☐ Thu ☐ Fri ☐ Sat ☐ Sun

Time:

Water Quality

Tank :

Water Type :

Temp: %

Change:

PH Level

Ammonia:

Nitrite

Nitrite

Dosing

Supplements	Quantity

Fish Info.

Fish Count :

Added Fish :

Lost Fish :

Feeding & Light

Feeding Time	Light Time
☐ AM/PM	ON AM/PM
☐ AM/PM	OFF AM/PM

Other Tests

Notes

Freshwater Aquarium Log Book

Date: / /

☐ Mon ☐ Tue ☐ Wed ☐ Thu ☐ Fri ☐ Sat ☐ Sun

Time:

Water Quality

Tank :

Water Type :

Temp: %

Change:

PH Level

Ammonia:

Nitrite

Nitrite

Dosing

Supplements	Quantity

Fish Info.

Fish Count :

Added Fish :

Lost Fish :

Feeding & Light

Feeding Time	Light Time
☐ AM/PM	ON AM/PM
☐ AM/PM	OFF AM/PM

Other Tests

Notes

Freshwater Aquarium Log Book

Date: / /

☐ Mon ☐ Tue ☐ Wed ☐ Thu ☐ Fri ☐ Sat ☐ Sun

Time:

Water Quality

Tank :

Water Type :

Temp: %

Change:

PH Level

Ammonia:

Nitrite

Nitrite

Dosing

Supplements	Quantity

Fish Info.

Fish Count :

Added Fish :

Lost Fish :

Feeding & Light

Feeding Time	Light Time
☐ AM/PM	ON AM/PM
☐ AM/PM	OFF AM/PM

Other Tests

Notes

Date: / /

☐ Mon ☐ Tue ☐ Wed ☐ Thu ☐ Fri ☐ Sat ☐ Sun

Time:

Water Quality

Tank :

Water Type :

Temp: %

Change:

PH Level

Ammonia:

Nitrite

Nitrite

Dosing

Supplements	Quantity

Freshwater Aquarium Log Book

Fish Info.

Fish Count :

Added Fish :

Lost Fish :

Feeding & Light

Feeding Time	Light Time
☐ AM/PM	ON AM/PM
☐ AM/PM	OFF AM/PM

Other Tests

Notes

Freshwater Aquarium Log Book

Date: / /

☐ Mon ☐ Tue ☐ Wed ☐ Thu ☐ Fri ☐ Sat ☐ Sun

Time:

Water Quality

Tank :

Water Type :

Temp: %

Change:

PH Level

Ammonia:

Nitrite

Nitrite

Dosing

Supplements	Quantity

Fish Info.

Fish Count :

Added Fish :

Lost Fish :

Feeding & Light

Feeding Time	Light Time
☐ AM/PM	ON AM/PM
☐ AM/PM	OFF AM/PM

Other Tests

Notes

Date: / /

☐ Mon ☐ Tue ☐ Wed ☐ Thu ☐ Fri ☐ Sat ☐ Sun

Time:

Water Quality

Tank :

Water Type :

Temp: %

Change:

PH Level

Ammonia:

Nitrite

Nitrite

Dosing

Supplements	Quantity

Freshwater Aquarium Log Book

Fish Info.

Fish Count :

Added Fish :

Lost Fish :

Feeding & Light

Feeding Time	Light Time
☐ AM/PM	ON AM/PM
☐ AM/PM	OFF AM/PM

Other Tests

Notes

Freshwater Aquarium Log Book

Date: / /

☐ Mon ☐ Tue ☐ Wed ☐ Thu ☐ Fri ☐ Sat ☐ Sun

Time:

Water Quality

Tank :

Water Type :

Temp: %

Change:

PH Level

Ammonia:

Nitrite

Nitrite

Dosing

Supplements	Quantity

Fish Info.

Fish Count :

Added Fish :

Lost Fish :

Feeding & Light

Feeding Time	Light Time
☐ AM/PM	ON AM/PM
☐ AM/PM	OFF AM/PM

Other Tests

Notes

Date: / /

☐ Mon ☐ Tue ☐ Wed ☐ Thu ☐ Fri ☐ Sat ☐ Sun

Time:

Water Quality

Tank :

Water Type :

Temp: %

Change:

PH Level

Ammonia:

Nitrite

Nitrite

Dosing

Supplements	Quantity

Freshwater Aquarium Log Book

Fish Info.

Fish Count :

Added Fish :

Lost Fish :

Feeding & Light

Feeding Time	Light Time
☐ AM/PM	ON AM/PM
☐ AM/PM	OFF AM/PM

Other Tests

Notes

Freshwater Aquarium Log Book

Date: / /

☐ Mon ☐ Tue ☐ Wed ☐ Thu ☐ Fri ☐ Sat ☐ Sun

Time:

Water Quality

Tank :

Water Type :

Temp: %

Change:

PH Level

Ammonia:

Nitrite

Nitrite

Dosing

Supplements	Quantity

Fish Info.

Fish Count :

Added Fish :

Lost Fish :

Feeding & Light

Feeding Time	Light Time
☐ AM/PM	ON AM/PM
☐ AM/PM	OFF AM/PM

Other Tests

Notes

Freshwater Aquarium Log Book

Date: / /

☐ Mon ☐ Tue ☐ Wed ☐ Thu ☐ Fri ☐ Sat ☐ Sun

Time:

Water Quality

Tank :

Water Type :

Temp: %

Change:

PH Level

Ammonia:

Nitrite

Nitrite

Dosing

Supplements	Quantity

Fish Info.

Fish Count :

Added Fish :

Lost Fish :

Feeding & Light

Feeding Time	Light Time
☐ AM/PM	ON AM/PM
☐ AM/PM	OFF AM/PM

Other Tests

Notes

Freshwater Aquarium Log Book

Date: / /

☐ Mon ☐ Tue ☐ Wed ☐ Thu ☐ Fri ☐ Sat ☐ Sun

Time:

Water Quality

Tank :

Water Type :

Temp: %

Change:

PH Level

Ammonia:

Nitrite

Nitrite

Dosing

Supplements	Quantity

Fish Info.

Fish Count :

Added Fish :

Lost Fish :

Feeding & Light

Feeding Time	Light Time
☐ AM/PM	ON AM/PM
☐ AM/PM	OFF AM/PM

Other Tests

Notes

Freshwater Aquarium Log Book

Date: / /

☐ Mon ☐ Tue ☐ Wed ☐ Thu ☐ Fri ☐ Sat ☐ Sun

Time:

Water Quality

Tank :

Water Type :

Temp: %

Change:

PH Level

Ammonia:

Nitrite

Nitrite

Dosing

Supplements	Quantity

Fish Info.

Fish Count :

Added Fish :

Lost Fish :

Feeding & Light

Feeding Time		Light Time	
☐	AM/PM	ON	AM/PM
☐	AM/PM	OFF	AM/PM

Other Tests

Notes

Date: / /

☐ Mon ☐ Tue ☐ Wed ☐ Thu ☐ Fri ☐ Sat ☐ Sun

Time:

Water Quality

Tank :

Water Type :

Temp: %

Change:

PH Level

Ammonia:

Nitrite

Nitrite

Dosing

Supplements	Quantity

Freshwater Aquarium Log Book

Fish Info.

Fish Count :

Added Fish :

Lost Fish :

Feeding & Light

Feeding Time	Light Time
☐ AM/PM	ON AM/PM
☐ AM/PM	OFF AM/PM

Other Tests

Notes

Freshwater Aquarium Log Book

Date: / /

☐ Mon ☐ Tue ☐ Wed ☐ Thu ☐ Fri ☐ Sat ☐ Sun

Time:

Water Quality

Tank :

Water Type :

Temp: %

Change:

PH Level

Ammonia:

Nitrite

Nitrite

Dosing

Supplements	Quantity

Fish Info.

Fish Count :

Added Fish :

Lost Fish :

Feeding & Light

Feeding Time	Light Time
☐ AM/PM	ON AM/PM
☐ AM/PM	OFF AM/PM

Other Tests

Notes

Date: / /

☐ Mon ☐ Tue ☐ Wed ☐ Thu ☐ Fri ☐ Sat ☐ Sun

Time:

Fish Info.

Fish Count :

Added Fish :

Lost Fish :

Water Quality

Tank :

Water Type :

Temp: %

Change:

PH Level

Ammonia:

Nitrite

Nitrite

Feeding & Light

Feeding Time	Light Time
☐ AM/PM	ON AM/PM
☐ AM/PM	OFF AM/PM

Freshwater Aquarium Log Book

Dosing

Supplements	Quantity

Other Tests

Notes

Freshwater Aquarium Log Book

Date: / /

☐ Mon ☐ Tue ☐ Wed ☐ Thu ☐ Fri ☐ Sat ☐ Sun

Time:

Water Quality

Tank :

Water Type :

Temp: %

Change:

PH Level

Ammonia:

Nitrite

Nitrite

Dosing

Supplements	Quantity

Fish Info.

Fish Count :

Added Fish :

Lost Fish :

Feeding & Light

Feeding Time	Light Time
☐ AM/PM	ON AM/PM
☐ AM/PM	OFF AM/PM

Other Tests

Notes

Date: / /

☐ Mon ☐ Tue ☐ Wed ☐ Thu ☐ Fri ☐ Sat ☐ Sun

Time:

Water Quality

Tank :

Water Type :

Temp: %

Change:

PH Level

Ammonia:

Nitrite

Nitrite

Dosing

Supplements	Quantity

Freshwater Aquarium Log Book

Fish Info.

Fish Count :

Added Fish :

Lost Fish :

Feeding & Light

Feeding Time	Light Time
☐ AM/PM	ON AM/PM
☐ AM/PM	OFF AM/PM

Other Tests

Notes

Freshwater Aquarium Log Book

Date: / /

☐ Mon ☐ Tue ☐ Wed ☐ Thu ☐ Fri ☐ Sat ☐ Sun

Time:

Water Quality

Tank :

Water Type :

Temp: %

Change:

PH Level

Ammonia:

Nitrite

Nitrite

Dosing

Supplements	Quantity

Fish Info.

Fish Count :

Added Fish :

Lost Fish :

Feeding & Light

Feeding Time	Light Time
☐ AM/PM	ON AM/PM
☐ AM/PM	OFF AM/PM

Other Tests

Notes

Date: / /

☐ Mon ☐ Tue ☐ Wed ☐ Thu ☐ Fri ☐ Sat ☐ Sun

Time:

Water Quality

Tank :

Water Type :

Temp: %

Change:

PH Level

Ammonia:

Nitrite

Nitrite

Dosing

Supplements	Quantity

Freshwater Aquarium Log Book

Fish Info.

Fish Count :

Added Fish :

Lost Fish :

Feeding & Light

Feeding Time	Light Time
☐ AM/PM	ON AM/PM
☐ AM/PM	OFF AM/PM

Other Tests

Notes

Date: / /

☐ Mon ☐ Tue ☐ Wed ☐ Thu ☐ Fri ☐ Sat ☐ Sun

Time:

Water Quality

Tank :

Water Type :

Temp: %

Change:

PH Level

Ammonia:

Nitrite

Nitrite

Dosing

Supplements	Quantity

Freshwater Aquarium Log Book

Fish Info.

Fish Count :

Added Fish :

Lost Fish :

Feeding & Light

Feeding Time	Light Time
☐ AM/PM	ON AM/PM
☐ AM/PM	OFF AM/PM

Other Tests

Notes

Freshwater Aquarium Log Book

Date: / /

☐ Mon ☐ Tue ☐ Wed ☐ Thu ☐ Fri ☐ Sat ☐ Sun

Time:

Water Quality

Tank :

Water Type :

Temp: %

Change:

PH Level

Ammonia:

Nitrite

Nitrite

Dosing

Supplements	Quantity

Fish Info.

Fish Count :

Added Fish :

Lost Fish :

Feeding & Light

Feeding Time	Light Time
☐ AM/PM	ON AM/PM
☐ AM/PM	OFF AM/PM

Other Tests

Notes

Date: / /

☐ Mon ☐ Tue ☐ Wed ☐ Thu ☐ Fri ☐ Sat ☐ Sun

Time:

Water Quality

Tank :

Water Type :

Temp: %

Change:

PH Level

Ammonia:

Nitrite

Nitrite

Dosing

Supplements	Quantity

Freshwater Aquarium Log Book

Fish Info.

Fish Count :

Added Fish :

Lost Fish :

Feeding & Light

Feeding Time	Light Time
☐ AM/PM	ON AM/PM
☐ AM/PM	OFF AM/PM

Other Tests

Notes

Date: / /

☐ Mon ☐ Tue ☐ Wed ☐ Thu ☐ Fri ☐ Sat ☐ Sun

Time:

Water Quality

Tank :

Water Type :

Temp: %

Change:

PH Level

Ammonia:

Nitrite

Nitrite

Dosing

Supplements	Quantity

Freshwater Aquarium Log Book

Fish Info.

Fish Count :

Added Fish :

Lost Fish :

Feeding & Light

Feeding Time	Light Time
☐ AM/PM	ON AM/PM
☐ AM/PM	OFF AM/PM

Other Tests

Notes

Freshwater Aquarium Log Book

Date: / /

☐ Mon ☐ Tue ☐ Wed ☐ Thu ☐ Fri ☐ Sat ☐ Sun

Time:

Fish Info.

Fish Count :

Added Fish :

Lost Fish :

Water Quality

Tank :

Water Type :

Temp: %

Change:

PH Level

Ammonia:

Nitrite

Nitrite

Feeding & Light

Feeding Time	Light Time
☐ AM/PM	ON AM/PM
☐ AM/PM	OFF AM/PM

Dosing

Supplements	Quantity

Other Tests

Notes

Date: / /

☐ Mon ☐ Tue ☐ Wed ☐ Thu ☐ Fri ☐ Sat ☐ Sun

Time:

Water Quality

Tank :

Water Type :

Temp: %

Change:

PH Level

Ammonia:

Nitrite

Nitrite

Dosing

Supplements	Quantity

Freshwater Aquarium Log Book

Fish Info.

Fish Count :

Added Fish :

Lost Fish :

Feeding & Light

Feeding Time	Light Time
☐ AM/PM	ON AM/PM
☐ AM/PM	OFF AM/PM

Other Tests

Notes

Freshwater Aquarium Log Book

Date: / /

☐ Mon ☐ Tue ☐ Wed ☐ Thu ☐ Fri ☐ Sat ☐ Sun

Time:

Water Quality

Tank :

Water Type :

Temp: %

Change:

PH Level

Ammonia:

Nitrite

Nitrite

Dosing

Supplements	Quantity

Fish Info.

Fish Count :

Added Fish :

Lost Fish :

Feeding & Light

Feeding Time	Light Time
☐ AM/PM	ON AM/PM
☐ AM/PM	OFF AM/PM

Other Tests

Notes

Freshwater Aquarium Log Book

Date: / /

☐ Mon ☐ Tue ☐ Wed ☐ Thu ☐ Fri ☐ Sat ☐ Sun

Time:

Water Quality

Tank :
Water Type :
Temp: %
Change:
PH Level
Ammonia:
Nitrite
Nitrite

Dosing

Supplements	Quantity

Fish Info.

Fish Count :
Added Fish :
Lost Fish :

Feeding & Light

Feeding Time	Light Time
☐ AM/PM	ON AM/PM
☐ AM/PM	OFF AM/PM

Other Tests

Notes

Date: / /

☐ Mon ☐ Tue ☐ Wed ☐ Thu ☐ Fri ☐ Sat ☐ Sun

Time:

Water Quality

Tank :

Water Type :

Temp: %

Change:

PH Level

Ammonia:

Nitrite

Nitrite

Dosing

Supplements	Quantity

Freshwater Aquarium Log Book

Fish Info.

Fish Count :

Added Fish :

Lost Fish :

Feeding & Light

Feeding Time	Light Time
☐ AM/PM	ON AM/PM
☐ AM/PM	OFF AM/PM

Other Tests

Notes

Freshwater Aquarium Log Book

Date: / /

☐ Mon ☐ Tue ☐ Wed ☐ Thu ☐ Fri ☐ Sat ☐ Sun

Time:

Water Quality

Tank :

Water Type :

Temp: %

Change:

PH Level

Ammonia:

Nitrite

Nitrite

Dosing

Supplements	Quantity

Fish Info.

Fish Count :

Added Fish :

Lost Fish :

Feeding & Light

Feeding Time	Light Time
☐ AM/PM	ON AM/PM
☐ AM/PM	OFF AM/PM

Other Tests

Notes

Date: / /

☐ Mon ☐ Tue ☐ Wed ☐ Thu ☐ Fri ☐ Sat ☐ Sun

Time:

Water Quality

Tank :

Water Type :

Temp: %

Change:

PH Level

Ammonia:

Nitrite

Nitrite

Dosing

Supplements	Quantity

Freshwater Aquarium Log Book

Fish Info.

Fish Count :

Added Fish :

Lost Fish :

Feeding & Light

Feeding Time	Light Time
☐ AM/PM	ON AM/PM
☐ AM/PM	OFF AM/PM

Other Tests

Notes

Freshwater Aquarium Log Book

Date: / /

☐ Mon ☐ Tue ☐ Wed ☐ Thu ☐ Fri ☐ Sat ☐ Sun

Time:

Water Quality

Tank :

Water Type :

Temp: %

Change:

PH Level

Ammonia:

Nitrite

Nitrite

Dosing

Supplements	Quantity

Fish Info.

Fish Count :

Added Fish :

Lost Fish :

Feeding & Light

Feeding Time	Light Time
☐ AM/PM	ON AM/PM
☐ AM/PM	OFF AM/PM

Other Tests

Notes

Date: / /

☐ Mon ☐ Tue ☐ Wed ☐ Thu ☐ Fri ☐ Sat ☐ Sun

Time:

Water Quality

Tank :

Water Type :

Temp: %

Change:

PH Level

Ammonia:

Nitrite

Nitrite

Dosing

Supplements	Quantity

Freshwater Aquarium Log Book

Fish Info.

Fish Count :

Added Fish :

Lost Fish :

Feeding & Light

Feeding Time	Light Time
☐ AM/PM	ON AM/PM
☐ AM/PM	OFF AM/PM

Other Tests

Notes

Date: / /

☐ Mon ☐ Tue ☐ Wed ☐ Thu ☐ Fri ☐ Sat ☐ Sun

Time:

Freshwater Aquarium Log Book

Water Quality

Tank :

Water Type :

Temp: %

Change:

PH Level

Ammonia:

Nitrite

Nitrite

Dosing

Supplements	Quantity

Fish Info.

Fish Count :

Added Fish :

Lost Fish :

Feeding & Light

Feeding Time	Light Time
☐ AM/PM	ON AM/PM
☐ AM/PM	OFF AM/PM

Other Tests

Notes

Freshwater Aquarium Log Book

Date: / /

☐ Mon ☐ Tue ☐ Wed ☐ Thu ☐ Fri ☐ Sat ☐ Sun

Time:

Water Quality

Tank :

Water Type :

Temp: %

Change:

PH Level

Ammonia:

Nitrite

Nitrite

Dosing

Supplements	Quantity

Fish Info.

Fish Count :

Added Fish :

Lost Fish :

Feeding & Light

Feeding Time	Light Time
☐ AM/PM	ON AM/PM
☐ AM/PM	OFF AM/PM

Other Tests

Notes

Date: / /

☐ Mon ☐ Tue ☐ Wed ☐ Thu ☐ Fri ☐ Sat ☐ Sun

Time:

Water Quality

Tank :

Water Type :

Temp: %

Change:

PH Level

Ammonia:

Nitrite

Nitrite

Dosing

Supplements	Quantity

Freshwater Aquarium Log Book

Fish Info.

Fish Count :

Added Fish :

Lost Fish :

Feeding & Light

Feeding Time	Light Time
☐ AM/PM	ON AM/PM
☐ AM/PM	OFF AM/PM

Other Tests

Notes

Date: / /

☐ Mon ☐ Tue ☐ Wed ☐ Thu ☐ Fri ☐ Sat ☐ Sun

Time:

Water Quality

Tank :

Water Type :

Temp: %

Change:

PH Level

Ammonia:

Nitrite

Nitrite

Dosing

Supplements	Quantity

Freshwater Aquarium Log Book

Fish Info.

Fish Count :

Added Fish :

Lost Fish :

Feeding & Light

Feeding Time	Light Time
☐ AM/PM	ON AM/PM
☐ AM/PM	OFF AM/PM

Other Tests

Notes

Freshwater Aquarium Log Book

Date: / /

☐ Mon ☐ Tue ☐ Wed ☐ Thu ☐ Fri ☐ Sat ☐ Sun

Time:

Water Quality

Tank :

Water Type :

Temp: %

Change:

PH Level

Ammonia:

Nitrite

Nitrite

Dosing

Supplements	Quantity

Fish Info.

Fish Count :

Added Fish :

Lost Fish :

Feeding & Light

Feeding Time	Light Time
☐ AM/PM	ON AM/PM
☐ AM/PM	OFF AM/PM

Other Tests

Notes

Date: / /

☐ Mon ☐ Tue ☐ Wed ☐ Thu ☐ Fri ☐ Sat ☐ Sun

Time:

Water Quality

Tank :

Water Type :

Temp: %

Change:

PH Level

Ammonia:

Nitrite

Nitrite

Dosing

Supplements	Quantity

Freshwater Aquarium Log Book

Fish Info.

Fish Count :

Added Fish :

Lost Fish :

Feeding & Light

Feeding Time	Light Time
☐ AM/PM	ON AM/PM
☐ AM/PM	OFF AM/PM

Other Tests

Notes

Date: / /

☐ Mon ☐ Tue ☐ Wed ☐ Thu ☐ Fri ☐ Sat ☐ Sun

Time:

Water Quality

Tank :
Water Type :
Temp: %
Change:
PH Level
Ammonia:
Nitrite
Nitrite

Dosing

Supplements	Quantity

Freshwater Aquarium Log Book

Fish Info.

Fish Count :
Added Fish :
Lost Fish :

Feeding & Light

Feeding Time	Light Time
☐ AM/PM	ON AM/PM
☐ AM/PM	OFF AM/PM

Other Tests

Notes

Freshwater Aquarium Log Book

Date: / /

☐ Mon ☐ Tue ☐ Wed ☐ Thu ☐ Fri ☐ Sat ☐ Sun

Time:

Water Quality

Tank :

Water Type :

Temp: %

Change:

PH Level

Ammonia:

Nitrite

Nitrite

Dosing

Supplements	Quantity

Fish Info.

Fish Count :

Added Fish :

Lost Fish :

Feeding & Light

Feeding Time	Light Time
☐ AM/PM	ON AM/PM
☐ AM/PM	OFF AM/PM

Other Tests

Notes

Freshwater Aquarium Log Book

Date: / /

☐ Mon ☐ Tue ☐ Wed ☐ Thu ☐ Fri ☐ Sat ☐ Sun

Time:

Water Quality

Tank :
Water Type :
Temp: %
Change:
PH Level
Ammonia:
Nitrite
Nitrite

Dosing

Supplements	Quantity

Fish Info.

Fish Count :
Added Fish :
Lost Fish :

Feeding & Light

Feeding Time	Light Time
☐ AM/PM	ON AM/PM
☐ AM/PM	OFF AM/PM

Other Tests

Notes

Freshwater Aquarium Log Book

Date: / /

☐ Mon ☐ Tue ☐ Wed ☐ Thu ☐ Fri ☐ Sat ☐ Sun

Time:

Water Quality

Tank :

Water Type :

Temp: %

Change:

PH Level

Ammonia:

Nitrite

Nitrite

Dosing

Supplements	Quantity

Fish Info.

Fish Count :

Added Fish :

Lost Fish :

Feeding & Light

Feeding Time	Light Time
☐ AM/PM	ON AM/PM
☐ AM/PM	OFF AM/PM

Other Tests

Notes

Date: / /

☐ Mon ☐ Tue ☐ Wed ☐ Thu ☐ Fri ☐ Sat ☐ Sun

Time:

Water Quality

Tank :

Water Type :

Temp: %

Change:

PH Level

Ammonia:

Nitrite

Nitrite

Dosing

Supplements	Quantity

Freshwater Aquarium Log Book

Fish Info.

Fish Count :

Added Fish :

Lost Fish :

Feeding & Light

Feeding Time	Light Time
☐ AM/PM	ON AM/PM
☐ AM/PM	OFF AM/PM

Other Tests

Notes

Date: / /

☐ Mon ☐ Tue ☐ Wed ☐ Thu ☐ Fri ☐ Sat ☐ Sun

Time:

Water Quality

Tank :

Water Type :

Temp: %

Change:

PH Level

Ammonia:

Nitrite

Nitrite

Dosing

Supplements	Quantity

Freshwater Aquarium Log Book

Fish Info.

Fish Count :

Added Fish :

Lost Fish :

Feeding & Light

Feeding Time	Light Time
☐ AM/PM	ON AM/PM
☐ AM/PM	OFF AM/PM

Other Tests

Notes

Date: / /

☐ Mon ☐ Tue ☐ Wed ☐ Thu ☐ Fri ☐ Sat ☐ Sun

Time:

Water Quality

Tank :

Water Type :

Temp: %

Change:

PH Level

Ammonia:

Nitrite

Nitrite

Dosing

Supplements	Quantity

Freshwater Aquarium Log Book

Fish Info.

Fish Count :

Added Fish :

Lost Fish :

Feeding & Light

Feeding Time	Light Time
☐ AM/PM	ON AM/PM
☐ AM/PM	OFF AM/PM

Other Tests

Notes

Freshwater Aquarium Log Book

Date: / /

☐ Mon ☐ Tue ☐ Wed ☐ Thu ☐ Fri ☐ Sat ☐ Sun

Time:

Water Quality

Tank :

Water Type :

Temp: %

Change:

PH Level

Ammonia:

Nitrite

Nitrite

Dosing

Supplements	Quantity

Fish Info.

Fish Count :

Added Fish :

Lost Fish :

Feeding & Light

Feeding Time	Light Time
☐ AM/PM	ON AM/PM
☐ AM/PM	OFF AM/PM

Other Tests

Notes

Freshwater Aquarium Log Book

Date: / /

☐ Mon ☐ Tue ☐ Wed ☐ Thu ☐ Fri ☐ Sat ☐ Sun

Time:

Water Quality

Tank :

Water Type :

Temp: %

Change:

PH Level

Ammonia:

Nitrite

Nitrite

Dosing

Supplements	Quantity

Fish Info.

Fish Count :

Added Fish :

Lost Fish :

Feeding & Light

Feeding Time	Light Time
☐ AM/PM	ON AM/PM
☐ AM/PM	OFF AM/PM

Other Tests

Notes

Date: / /

☐ Mon ☐ Tue ☐ Wed ☐ Thu ☐ Fri ☐ Sat ☐ Sun

Time:

Water Quality

Tank :

Water Type :

Temp: %

Change:

PH Level

Ammonia:

Nitrite

Nitrite

Dosing

Supplements	Quantity

Freshwater Aquarium Log Book

Fish Info.

Fish Count :

Added Fish :

Lost Fish :

Feeding & Light

Feeding Time	Light Time
☐ AM/PM	ON AM/PM
☐ AM/PM	OFF AM/PM

Other Tests

Notes

Date: / /

☐ Mon ☐ Tue ☐ Wed ☐ Thu ☐ Fri ☐ Sat ☐ Sun

Time:

Water Quality

Tank :

Water Type :

Temp: %

Change:

PH Level

Ammonia:

Nitrite

Nitrite

Dosing

Supplements	Quantity

Freshwater Aquarium Log Book

Fish Info.

Fish Count :

Added Fish :

Lost Fish :

Feeding & Light

Feeding Time	Light Time
☐ AM/PM	ON AM/PM
☐ AM/PM	OFF AM/PM

Other Tests

Notes

Date: / /

☐ Mon ☐ Tue ☐ Wed ☐ Thu ☐ Fri ☐ Sat ☐ Sun

Time:

Water Quality

Tank :

Water Type :

Temp: %

Change:

PH Level

Ammonia:

Nitrite

Nitrite

Dosing

Supplements	Quantity

Freshwater Aquarium Log Book

Fish Info.

Fish Count :

Added Fish :

Lost Fish :

Feeding & Light

Feeding Time	Light Time
☐ AM/PM	ON AM/PM
☐ AM/PM	OFF AM/PM

Other Tests

Notes

Date: / /

☐ Mon ☐ Tue ☐ Wed ☐ Thu ☐ Fri ☐ Sat ☐ Sun

Time:

Water Quality

Tank :

Water Type :

Temp: %

Change:

PH Level

Ammonia:

Nitrite

Nitrite

Dosing

Supplements	Quantity

Freshwater Aquarium Log Book

Fish Info.

Fish Count :

Added Fish :

Lost Fish :

Feeding & Light

Feeding Time	Light Time
☐ AM/PM	ON AM/PM
☐ AM/PM	OFF AM/PM

Other Tests

Notes

Freshwater Aquarium Log Book

Date: / /

☐ Mon ☐ Tue ☐ Wed ☐ Thu ☐ Fri ☐ Sat ☐ Sun

Time:

Water Quality

Tank :

Water Type :

Temp: %

Change:

PH Level

Ammonia:

Nitrite

Nitrite

Dosing

Supplements	Quantity

Fish Info.

Fish Count :

Added Fish :

Lost Fish :

Feeding & Light

Feeding Time	Light Time
☐ AM/PM	ON AM/PM
☐ AM/PM	OFF AM/PM

Other Tests

Notes

Printed in Great Britain
by Amazon

77230430R00075